Famous Childhoods

Ludwig van
BEETHOVEN

Barrie Carson Turner

Chrysalis Education

US publication copyright © 2003 Chrysalis Education.

International copyright reserved in all countries.
No part of this book may be reproduced in any
form without written permission from the publisher.

Distributed in the United States by
Smart Apple Media
1980 Lookout Drive
North Mankato, MN 56003

Copyright © Chrysalis Books PLC 2003
Text by Barrie Carson Turner

ISBN 1-59389-112-1

Library of Congress Control Number: 2003104921

Editorial Manager: Joyce Bentley
Senior Editor: Sarah Nunn
Picture Researcher: Jenny Barlow
Produced by Tall Tree Ltd
Editor: Jon Richards
Designer: Ed Simkins
Consultant: Yvonne Dix

Printed in China

10 9 8 7 6 5 4 3 2 1

CONTENTS

THE BEETHOVEN FAMILY

The Beethoven family lived in Bonn, Germany. The family name, van Beethoven, came from Belgium and had been brought to Germany by grandfather Louis Beethoven, who was the first musician in the family. He was a singer and had an extremely important job as director of music for the local governor of the area, the elector of Cologne.

◀ *Johann van Beethoven (c.1740-1792) also taught the violin and keyboard.*

LUDWIG'S FATHER

Father Johann was a singer at the electoral court, but, unlike Louis, he was not made director of music.

A GENIUS IN THE MAKING

Ludwig grew up surrounded by the sound of singing.
He went on to write almost 100 songs and made many
arrangements of folk songs.

LUDWIG'S HOME

The house where the Beethovens lived was in a respectable part of Bonn. The building was owned by a well-to-do gold-lace maker.

◀ *515 Bonngasse, the house in which Ludwig was born.*

▼ *A picture of the city of Bonn at the time of Ludwig's birth in 1770.*

BONN

The city of Bonn stands on one of the world's great waterways, the Rhine. For hundreds of years, the river has brought trade and travelers to the city.

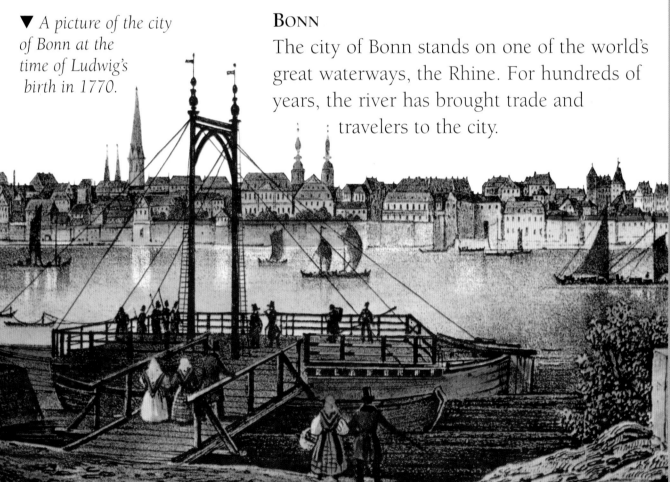

LUDWIG IS BORN

L udwig van Beethoven was born on December 16, 1770. He was the second of seven children born to the Beethovens, but only he and two younger brothers, Caspar Carl and Nikolaus Johann, survived into adulthood. The early years of life were very hazardous in Ludwig's day, and childbirth was dangerous for both mother and baby, because medical knowledge was poor.

THE CHRISTENING
Ludwig was named after his grandfather and was christened the day after he was born, as was the custom in the Catholic Church. The christening feast was paid for by Frau Baums, Ludwig's godmother.

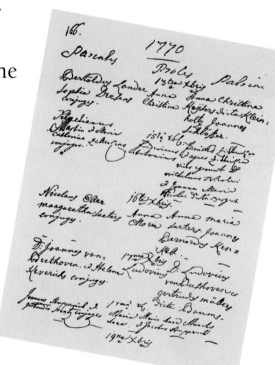

▲ *Ludwig's christening document, recording the occasion at the church of St. Remigius, Bonn.*

A GENIUS IN THE MAKING

Through his father, Ludwig learned to enjoy every kind of music. As a composer, Ludwig wrote for almost every instrument. He even wrote some pieces for a mechanical clock!

LUDWIG'S BIRTHPLACE

Ludwig's parents were not rich and their home was in a boarding house. Their rooms were inexpensive because they were high up under the roof at the back of the building. It was here that Ludwig spent the first years of his life.

◀ *Today, the Beethoven family rooms have been turned into a Beethoven museum, and house the piano that Ludwig owned.*

THE ELECTORAL PALACE

The local rulers, the electors, lived in the Electoral Palace. Wealth, grandeur, and beautiful buildings were important to the electors, as were music and culture.

▼ *The Beethoven children often played in the gardens of the Electoral Palace.*

MUSIC LESSONS

Johann wanted his son to become a musician. When Ludwig was four or five, Johann began teaching him piano and violin. He also had special plans for Ludwig. A few years earlier, a young Austrian boy called Wolfgang Amadeus Mozart had traveled Europe, entertaining the nobility with his astonishing keyboard playing. Surely Ludwig could also do this?

THE MOZARTS

Wolfgang Amadeus Mozart had a sister, Nannerl, who was almost as talented as her brother. The children performed together at the royal courts of Europe during tours in the 1760s.

▼ *Wolfgang Amadeus Mozart playing the harpsichord, accompanied by his father and sister.*

MUSIC FOR THE RICH

Playing an instrument or being able to sing was considered an essential skill in fashionable society. Johann wanted his son to be a music teacher because a good teacher could always earn a decent salary.

◀ *Wealthy families always employed a music teacher.*

AT SCHOOL

In 1777, Ludwig started his education at a school on the same street where the family lived. But Ludwig did not do very well in his school studies. His father Johann, however, thought that his music lessons at home were far more important than his lessons at school.

▲ *A school in 18th-century Germany.*

A GENIUS IN THE MAKING

Johann always insisted that Ludwig worked hard at his piano practice. Ludwig composed many pieces for the piano, including chamber music, short solo pieces, and 32 piano sonatas.

Playing in Public

When Ludwig was seven, Johann felt that the time had come to introduce his son to the world. After all, Wolfgang Mozart had now grown up, so it was the perfect time to introduce another brilliant child performer. So Johann took Ludwig to play for the royal court in Bonn.

▲ *Cologne at the time of Ludwig's visit.*

Cologne

Six months later, in March 1778, Ludwig performed in Cologne. Here, Johann played a trick on the audience. He told them that Ludwig was only six years old when in fact he was seven! He hoped that his audience would be even more impressed with his son's playing.

A GENIUS IN THE MAKING
According to Johann, Ludwig played various concertos and trios at his first public concert. Ludwig went on to compose his first piano concerto when he was 14 and a further five concertos as an adult.

TWO NEW INSTRUMENTS

Ludwig now had a new piano teacher, Tobias Pfeiffer, who was a lodger in the Beethoven household. Ludwig also started lessons on two new instruments—the viola and the organ.

▲ *The viola is a string instrument that looks similar to a violin but is larger and has a deeper sound.*

KEYBOARD AND STRINGS

In Ludwig's day it was essential for all music students to play a string instrument and the keyboard (piano, organ, and harpsichord), since almost every piece of music required one of these instruments.

▲ *An 18th-century chamber concert with a harpsichord accompanying strings and woodwind.*

FAMILY PROBLEMS

T he Beethoven household was not always a happy one. According to stories told by their landlord, the children were often left in the care of servants and their father was very strict. A fellow school pupil of Ludwig recorded that the Beethoven brothers always appeared unkempt and neglected.

TOO MUCH TO DRINK

Although Johann was a serious musician, he also liked to have a good time. By 1777, however, he was close to becoming an alcoholic.

▲ *Johann especially enjoyed drinking in the local taverns of Bonn.*

MONEY PROBLEMS

During these early years, times were hard for the Beethovens. Johann's voice was not as good as it had been, and his earnings fell. The family had to pawn some things to make ends meet.

◀ *A pawn shop is a place where people can sell their possessions.*

LUDWIG'S MOTHER

We do not know if Maria Magdalena was musical. But we do know that Ludwig owed much of his early musical encouragement to her. Even though times had been difficult as a child, Ludwig always spoke of her as a "good, kind mother," and his "best friend."

▶ *With her near-alcoholic husband, Maria Magdalena Beethoven (1746-1787) had a difficult time raising her family.*

A GENIUS IN THE MAKING

The piano was Ludwig's favorite instrument, but the violin ran a close second. Ludwig wrote a violin concerto, a concerto for piano, violin, and cello, and ten violin sonatas.

AN IMPORTANT INFLUENCE

Johann was always on the lookout for good teachers for Ludwig, especially ones with influence in Bonn's musical world or at the royal court. People with influence would be able to help his son's musical career. In 1779, a new theatrical company arrived in Bonn, and it was headed by an impressive music director.

NEW TEACHER

The music director who so impressed Johann was called Christian Gottlob Neefe. Johann met the newcomer and asked if he would teach his son. Neefe agreed and became Ludwig's first great musical influence.

▶ *Christian Gottlob Neefe (1748-1798). As a young adult, Beethoven wrote to Neefe, saying, "if ever I become a great man, yours shall be a share of the credit."*

A GENIUS IN THE MAKING

Through Johann Sebastian Bach's pieces, Ludwig developed a love of fugues and used them in many of his compositions. His Grosse Fuge ("Great Fugue") is for string quartet and dates from 1825-1826.

JOHANN SEBASTIAN BACH

Ludwig's new teacher taught him the piano and general musicianship and gave him his first composition lessons. His teacher admired the works of the German composer Johann Sebastian Bach, and used the composer's books of preludes and fugues as practice pieces for his pupils.

◀ *Johann Sebastian Bach (1685-1750) wrote an enormous amount of music for the keyboard.*

PRELUDES AND FUGUES

Prelude in C is the easiest to play of all Bach's preludes and fugues. Most of the other pieces are difficult, some extremely so, yet Ludwig always enjoyed the challenge of playing them. Bach called his two books of 48 preludes and fugues the *Well-Tempered Clavier*, meaning the "well-tuned keyboard."

▶ *Prelude in C is the first piece in Bach's preludes and fugues. He wrote these pieces for his pupils.*

THE END OF SCHOOL

In 1781, Ludwig left school at the age of 11. He had learned a little Latin and French, but, it seems, very little else. Herr Neefe introduced him to subjects such as literature and philosophy, but his German spelling and grammar and his mathematics were weak, and remained so for the rest of his life.

▶ *One of Ludwig's childhood pieces, written at the age of 15.*

MESSY WRITER
Throughout his life, Ludwig was a messy writer. Many of his letters and manuscripts, especially those from his younger years, are full of mistakes and corrections.

A GENIUS IN THE MAKING
Ludwig composed only one piece for organ solo, Fugue in D, written when he was 13. But it is possible that other pieces were written and lost. The organ also appears in some of his church music.

NEW ORGAN TEACHER

The year Ludwig left school, he had a new organ teacher, a Franciscan monk called Willibald Koch. Ludwig found his teacher extremely capable and was especially pleased when Brother Willibald referred to Ludwig as his "assistant."

▲ *The order of Franciscan monks, to which Father Koch belonged, was founded by St. Francis of Assisi.*

MINORITE ORGAN

Ludwig was offered a small but regular organist's position, playing for mass each day at the Minorite Monastery in Bonn, at six in the morning! It enabled Ludwig to help out a little with the family expenses.

▶ *The organ in the Minorite Monastery that Ludwig played each day.*

THE PUBLISHED COMPOSER

The years 1782 and 1783 were great years for Ludwig. In 1782, one of his piano compositions, a set of variations, appeared in print. It's not surprising that Herr Neefe was pleased with his pupil's progress. He was so pleased, in fact, that he wrote an article for Cramer's music magazine, a very respected publication, telling its readers about his pupil. "Ludwig van Beethoven could become a second Mozart," the article said.

JOSEPH HAYDN

Sets of variations for piano were very popular in Ludwig's day. They allowed the composer to show how much could be done with only one melody, just by changing it—making variations—and presenting it in different ways. The master of this technique was the composer Joseph Haydn.

▶ *Joseph Haydn (1732-1809), who later became Ludwig's teacher.*

THREE SONATAS

A few months after the publication of his piano variations, the 12-year-old Ludwig published three more piano pieces. He dedicated these works to the Elector Maximilian Friedrich of Cologne.

▶ *Maximilian Friedrich, Elector of Cologne from 1761 to 1784.*

▲ *Front page from the sonatas dedicated to Maximilian Friedrich.*

THE ELECTOR OF COLOGNE

It was a huge honor for Ludwig when the elector accepted the dedication. Music was important to Maximilian Friedrich, and he enjoyed playing it as well as attending concerts.

A GENIUS IN THE MAKING

Ludwig composed a total of 20 sets of piano variations. He even wrote a set of variations on the British national anthem, God save the King.

A VISIT TO THE NETHERLANDS

Ludwig was very happy being a composer. But his father still hoped that his son would become a performer and travel Europe, bringing fame and fortune to the family as Wolfgang Amadeus Mozart had done.

A TRIP TO ROTTERDAM

In the fall of 1783, an opportunity to travel presented itself. The Beethovens were invited to Rotterdam, the Netherlands, for a vacation. The invitation came from the sister of Franz Rovantini, Ludwig's recently deceased violin and viola teacher.

▲ *At the mouth of the Rhine, Rotterdam was a gateway for trade into Europe.*

◀ Passenger and trade vessels on the Rhine in the 18th century.

BOAT TRAVEL

Ludwig and his mother accepted the invitation to travel to the Netherlands and made the journey by boat, traveling down the Rhine. Ludwig believed the trip would be a good chance to show off his musical skills.

DUTCH CONCERTS

Ludwig played in several private houses during his trip to the Netherlands, but he received very little money in payment. Back in Germany, he scorned the stinginess of the Dutch. "I will never go back to Holland," he said. And he never did.

▶ A chamber concert in 18th-century Amsterdam.

A GENIUS IN THE MAKING

Ludwig knew that music must have variety to hold an audience's attention. His Moonlight sonata begins with slow, dreamy music, followed by a jaunty dance melody, and then stormy, fast music.

PROFESSIONAL MUSICIAN

Christian Gottlob Neefe placed great trust in his pupil as a performing musician. At just 11 years old, Ludwig had already been left in charge as court organist when his teacher was required elsewhere on business.

HARPSICHORD PLAYER

Now 13, another opportunity arose for Ludwig when Herr Neefe was overburdened with work. The musician in charge of court music was away, and Herr Neefe asked Ludwig to help out by becoming deputy harpsichordist and accompanist in the electoral theater orchestra.

▲ *As deputy harpsichordist, Ludwig played the harpsichord during opera performances.*

CHRISTOPH WILLIBALD GLUCK

In his position as keyboard player in the theater orchestra, Ludwig performed in most of the popular operas of his day. These included those by the respected German composer, Christoph Willibald Gluck.

◀ *Christoph Willibald Gluck (1714-1787), wrote many operas, including* Orpheus and Euridice *and* Alceste.

NEW INSTRUMENTS

Accompanying an orchestra meant that Ludwig was in close contact with a whole range of instruments. These included brass instruments such as horns, as well as woodwind, strings, and sometimes percussion. Such exciting music was perfect for a young composer like Ludwig who was learning how to write for them.

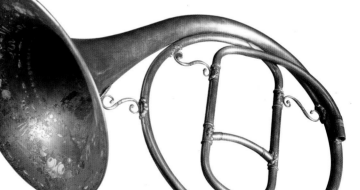

▼ *An 18th-century horn.*

A GENIUS IN THE MAKING

By playing in an orchestra, Ludwig learned a lot about writing orchestral music. His ninth symphony used the biggest orchestra of its day.

THE ASSISTANT ORGANIST

Now that he was deputizing for his teacher, Ludwig thought he should be entitled to a little pay. With this in mind, he suggested to the court that he be made official assistant organist, and he was! But a few weeks later, Elector Maximilian Friedrich died without having agreed on Ludwig's salary.

NEW EMPLOYER

Luckily, the new elector, Maximilian Franz honored Ludwig's appointment. What's more, duties for the new position were light and left plenty of time for composition and study, and time too for Ludwig to take on his first piano pupils.

▶ *Maximilian Franz succeeded Maximilian Friedrich and ruled from 1784 to 1801.*

A GENIUS IN THE MAKING

At court, and through his organist jobs, Ludwig was learning about church music. One piece of church music took him four years to write—his Missa Solemnis ("Solemn Mass"), which he called his greatest work.

MASTERING THE ORGAN

Ludwig had been studying the organ now for several years. He knew that to be a fully professional musician it was essential to master this instrument. However, he was already a skilled performer.

◀ *An organist in the 18th century could earn a good living.*

EARLY PORTRAIT

The Beethovens were poor, and Johann did not have the money to commission expensive family portraits. As an adult, however, Ludwig could afford to have a great many portraits and sketches made of himself.

▶ *At some point in Ludwig's childhood, this silhouette portrait was drawn of the young composer. However, there are no records of who the artist was or when the portrait was done.*

A MEETING WITH MOZART

Ludwig's compositions were becoming longer and more mature, and he had already written a concerto for piano and orchestra. Through his work at the court, he met many professional composers and musicians of all kinds, and learned much from them.

COUNT VON WALDSTEIN

Ludwig became friends with the rich Count von Waldstein. Count von Waldstein and Ludwig often played music together, and the count soon became aware of his young friend's extraordinary musical skills. He gave Ludwig encouragement as well as important financial support.

◀ *Count von Waldstein (1762-1823) was eight years older than Ludwig, as well as an amateur musician and a close friend of the elector.*

A GENIUS IN THE MAKING

All composers learn by meeting other composers and listening to their music. Ludwig had lessons from Joseph Haydn and dedicated three piano sonatas to him in appreciation for the help the elder composer had given.

MEETING MOZART

Exciting things were now happening for 16-year-old Ludwig. Herr Neefe felt that it was time for his student to study in Vienna, and who better to study with than the great Wolfgang Amadeus Mozart! So plans were made and, as a surprise bonus, the elector agreed to fund the visit.

▶ *Wolfgang Amadeus Mozart (1756-1791) was now at the peak of his success as a composer.*

VIENNA

Vienna was the capital of Austria and one of the greatest musical centers in Europe. But although Ludwig met Mozart, his visit to the capital was cut short as his mother was ill and he was needed at home.

▼ *Musicians were drawn to Vienna to meet each other and gain inspiration from hearing one another's music.*

Ludwig's Legacy

Beethoven's mother died a few weeks after his return to Bonn. Ludwig was just 17 years old. But within five years he was back in Vienna, where he spent the rest of his life working as a composer.

Hearing loss

From the age of 30, Beethoven suffered from increasing hearing loss. Eventually, he became totally deaf. But this did not stop him from composing—like all composers, he was able to write music "in his head" without needing to play it. It did mean, however, that he lived his last years in total silence. He was unable to hear any of his own music, while his friends had to write down everything they said to him.

▲ *Ludwig lived to the age of 56.*

▲ *Ludwig's signature.*

DEATH OF THE COMPOSER

Ludwig van Beethoven died on March 26, 1827. His music has influenced composers for two centuries, and its influence is now stretching into a third.

▶ *Ludwig's statue in Bonn was unveiled during a grand Beethoven festival in 1845, nearly 20 years after the composer's death.*

─────── *A GENIUS IN THE MAKING* ───────

Ludwig wrote symphonies, concertos, chamber music, piano music, choral works, the opera Fidelio, songs, and many other shorter pieces for a variety of muscial instruments.

GLOSSARY

CHAMBER MUSIC
Music written for a small group of musicians and instruments.

CONCERTO
A piece usually for one instrument with orchestra. It is made up of sections called movements.

FUGUE
A piece of music, usually written for keyboard, in which a tune is played by each hand alternately. In a fugue for instruments, the tune is passed between the different instruments.

MANUSCRIPT
A piece of music that has been copied or written out by hand.

MASS
The service of the Roman Catholic church that is usually set to music.

NATIONAL ANTHEM
A song chosen to represent a country that is sung or played at important events.

OPERA
A musical play in which the actors sing their parts and are accompanied by an orchestra.

ORCHESTRA
A large group of instruments playing together.

PERCUSSION
Instruments, such as drums, that are struck, shaken, or rubbed to make their sounds.

PRELUDE
A piece, usually for the keyboard, often used to introduce another piece, such as a fugue.

SONATA
A piece normally made up of several sections, called movements, and written for piano, or one instrument with piano.

STRING QUARTET
Music written for two violins, a viola, and a cello to play together.

SYMPHONY
A long piece of music for an orchestra that is usually made up of four sections called movements.

VARIATIONS
The same melody presented in several different ways.

INDEX